W9-BYR-157

VIKINGS

BARBARIANS!
VIKINGS

KATHRYN HINDS

MARSHALL CAVENDISH · BENCHMARK · NEW YORK

In memory of my grandfathers, Frederick Fernquist and Donald Lupton

THE AUTHOR AND PUBLISHER SPECIALLY WISH TO THANK OREN FALK,
ASSISTANT PROFESSOR OF HISTORY AT CORNELL UNIVERSITY,
FOR HIS INVALUABLE HELP IN REVIEWING THE MANUSCRIPT OF THIS BOOK.

Marshall Cavendish Benchmark 99 White Plains Road Tarrytown, New York 10591
www.marshallcavendish.us
Text copyright © 2010 by Marshall Cavendish Corporation Map copyright © 2010 by Mike Reagan

All Internet sites were available and accurate when this book was sent to press.

LIBRARY OF CONGRESS CATALOGING-IN-PUBLICATION DATA
Hinds, Kathryn, 1962-
Vikings / by Kathryn Hinds.
p. cm. — (Barbarians!)
Includes bibliographical references and index.
Summary: "A history of the Viking Age, from about 793 to 1066"—Provided by publisher.
ISBN 978-0-7614-4074-1
1. Vikings—Juvenile literature. 2. Northmen—Juvenile literature. 3. Vikings. 4. Northmen.
I. Title. DL65.H565 2010   948'.022—dc22   2008039052

EDITOR: Joyce Stanton PUBLISHER: Michelle Bisson ART DIRECTOR: Anahid Hamparian
SERIES DESIGNER: Michael Nelson

Images provided by Rose Corbett Gordon, Art Editor of Mystic CT, from the following sources: Cover: The Granger Collection, NY Back cover: Gianni Dagli Orti/Corbis Page 1: British Museum/Art Resource, NY; pages 2-3: Christopher Wood Gallery, London/Bridgeman Art Library; page 6: Arni Magnusson Institute, Reykjavik, Iceland/Bridgeman Art Library; page 8: Delaware Art Museum, Wilmington/Bridgeman Art Library; page 10: British Library/HIP/Art Resource, NY; pages 11, 16, 38, 39: Private Collection/Bridgeman Art Library; page 15: Nationalmuseum, Stockholm/Bridgeman Art Library; page 17: The Granger Collection, NY; page 18: Erich Lessing/Art Resource, NY; pages 19, 71: The Art Archive/Historiska Muséet Stockholm/Gianni Dagli Orti; pages 21, 26, 40: Mary Evans Picture Library/Edwin Wallace/The Image Works; page 22: Dave G. Houser/Corbis; page 24: The Pierpont Morgan Library/Art Resource, NY; page 27: Stefano Bianchetti/Corbis; page 29: Royal Library, Copenhagen/Bridgeman Art Library; page 30: Houses of Parliament, Westminster, London/Bridgeman Art Library; pages 32, 56: Private Collection/Bridgeman Art Library; page 33: The Art Archive/Bibliothèque des Arts Décoratifs Paris/Gianni Dagli Orti; page 34: Scala/Art Resource, NY; pages 37, 64, 65: Werner Forman/Corbis; page 41: Ted Spiegel/Corbis; page 43: National Museums of Scotland/Bridgeman Art Library; page 44: Greg Probst/Corbis; page 45: Tim Thompson/Corbis; page 46: Nasjonalgalleriet, Oslo/Bridgeman Art Library; page 47: PoodlesRock/Corbis; pages 48, 50, 62, Mary Evans Picture Library/The Image Works; page 51: Archives Charmet/Bridgeman Art Library; page 52: Bettmann/Corbis; page 54: Werner Forman Archive/Biblioteca Nacional, Madrid/The Image Works; page 58: State Russian Museum, St. Petersburg/Bridgeman Art Library; page 60: Werner Forman/Topham/The Image Works; page 63: The Art Archive/British Library; pages 68, 69: The Art Archive/Musée de la Tapisserie Bayeux/Gianni Dagli Orti.

Printed in Malaysia
135642

cover: *The First Cargo,* painted in 1910 by N. C. Wyeth to illustrate a story by Sir Arthur Conan Doyle
half-title page: A seventh-century helmet found in a royal grave in England. It was probably either made in Scandinavia or inspired by Scandinavian armor.
title page: A dramatic though fanciful painting of a Viking fleet by an early twentieth-century English artist
back cover: An eleventh-century English ship built in the Viking style, portrayed in the Bayeux Tapestry

CONTENTS

WHO WERE THE BARBARIANS?

THE WORD *BARBARIAN* WAS COINED BY THE ANCIENT GREEKS and picked up by the Romans, imitating the sounds of languages they found incomprehensible. Soon, though, barbarians came to be thought of not just as peoples unfamiliar with the languages and customs of Greece and Rome, but as wild, uncivilized, uncultured peoples. This stereotype has largely endured to the present day, and the barbarian label has been applied to a variety of peoples from many parts of Europe and Asia. For example, to the medieval European farmers and town dwellers who inherited Roman civilization, no one could have been more barbaric than the Vikings.

above: Egil Skallagrimsson, tenth-century Viking poet

The barbarians, of course, did not think of themselves this way. They had rich cultures of their own, as even some ancient writers realized. Great Greek and Roman historians such as Herodotus and Tacitus investigated and described their customs, sometimes even holding them up as examples for the people of their own sophisticated societies. Moreover, the relationships between the barbarians and civilization were varied and complex. Barbarians are most famous for raiding and invading, and these were certainly among their activities. But often the barbarians were peaceable neighbors and close allies, trading with the more settled peoples and even serving them as soldiers and contributing to their societies in other ways.

Our information about the barbarians comes from a variety of sources: archaeology, language studies, ancient and medieval historians, and later literature. Unfortunately, though, we generally have few records in the barbarians' own words, since many of these peoples did not leave much written material. Instead we frequently learn about them from the writings of civilizations who thought of them as strange and usually inferior, and often as enemies. But modern scholars, like detectives, have been sifting through the evidence to learn more and more about these peoples and the compelling roles they have played in the history of Europe, Asia, and even Africa. Now it's our turn to look beyond the borders of the familiar "great civilizations" of the past and meet the barbarians.

INTRODUCING the VIKINGS

O FF THE COAST OF THE MEDIEVAL ENGLISH KINGDOM OF Northumbria lay Lindisfarne. This island was home to one of the most influential monasteries in Christian Europe. Here monks produced beautiful books: copies of the Bible and lives of the saints and works of great learning on many subjects. Here, too, was the tomb of Saint Cuthbert, a renowned holy man. Generations of Northumbrian kings were also buried at Lindisfarne, which they had honored as their special church. Both from royal gifts and large landholdings (on the mainland as well as the island), the monastery enjoyed great wealth. The monks worshipped at altars adorned with precious metalwork, pursuing their prayers in peace and plenty.

Then, in 793, as recorded in an early English history called the *Anglo-Saxon Chronicle*,

Dire portents appeared over Northumbria and sorely frightened the people. They consisted of immense whirlwinds and flashes

A page from the Lindisfarne Gospels, one of the precious books produced by the monks of Lindisfarne before the monastery was raided by Vikings

of lightning, and fiery dragons were seen flying through the air. A great famine immediately followed those signs, and a little after that in the same year, on 8 June, the ravages of heathen men miserably destroyed God's church on Lindisfarne, with plunder and slaughter.

Another early chronicle identified the raiders and elaborated on their actions: "The pagans from the northern region came with a naval armament to Britain, like stinging hornets, and overran the country in all directions, like fierce wolves, plundering, tearing, and killing not only sheep and oxen, but priests . . . and choirs of monks and nuns."

The fact that the raiders were not Christians, targeted a holy place, and harmed people dedicated to religion made the attack especially shocking. Moreover, no one had dreamed that the island monastery could be vulnerable to such an assault. The Northumbrian scholar Alcuin, writing shortly after the event, summed up its impact: "Never before has such terror appeared in Britain as we have now suffered from a pagan race; nor was it thought that such an inroad from the sea could be made." But making "inroads from the sea" was something at which these northern people, whom we know as the Vikings, excelled.

THE LANDS OF THE NORTH

The Vikings, also known as the Norse or Northmen, came from what are now Denmark, Norway, and Sweden, nations that only took shape later during the medieval period. They are located in the northern

European region known as Scandinavia, which occupies two peninsulas and hundreds of islands. One peninsula, Jutland, sticks up like a thumb from what is now Germany and commands the passage from the North Sea to the Baltic Sea. Jutland's land is flat and rich-soiled. During the time of the Vikings, much of it was covered by forests of deciduous trees such as oak, and there were many bogs and marshes. The Scandinavian Peninsula (from which the whole region takes its name) hangs down from the north, dividing the Baltic from the North Atlantic. The terrain ranges from fertile lowlands in the southeast to rugged mountains in the west, where the Norwegian coast is indented with hundreds of fjords. Deciduous trees grow in the south, giving way to mixed deciduous and evergreen forests and then to taiga, where only cone-bearing evergreens grow, and finally to arctic tundra in the north.

Two major groups lived (and still live) in Scandinavia. One was the Saami, who tended to be nomadic, following reindeer herds and other animals that they depended on for their survival. During the Middle Ages they inhabited a larger region than they now occupy, which is in the north of Norway, Sweden, Finland, and Russia. Their language was related to Hungarian and Finnish; medieval Scandinavian writers referred to them as Finns. The people we typically think of as Scandinavians spoke a language related to English and German, Old Norse. (This language was the direct ancestor of modern Icelandic, Danish, Norwegian, and Swedish.) Their lifestyle was a mainly settled one based on farming.

A Saami woman milks a reindeer. The Saami have a long tradition of reindeer hunting and herding.

GREENLAND

ICELAND

LANGANES

SNAEFELLSNES

HORN

WESTERN SETTLEMENT

REYKJANES

THINGVELLIR

MIDDLE SETTLEMENT

FAE

EASTERN SETTLEMENT

HEBR

NORTH
ATLANTIC

MARKLAND?

IREL

LIMERICK

L'ANSE AUX MEADOWS

VINLAND?

N

LISBO

THE WORLD
OF THE VIKINGS

MILES

0   200

NORWAY

SWEDEN

FINLAND

BALTIC SEA

STAD

UPPSALA
OSEBERG
GOKSTAD
BIRKA

STARAYA LADOGA

LANDS

NEYS

NORTH
SEA

DENMARK

GOTLAND

NOVGOROD

RUSSIA

BULGAR

SCOTLAND

LINDISFARNE

JARROW

IAN

YORK

HEDEBY

HAMBURG

WALES

ENGLAND

FRISIA

LONDON

DORESTAD

KIEV

DNIEPER

VOLGA

ROUEN

NORMANDY

FRANKIA

PARIS

RITTANY

SEINE

LOIRE

RHÔNE

CAMARGUE

PISA

ROME

ITALY

BLACK SEA

CASPIAN SEA

CONSTANTINOPLE

BAKU

BERIA

CÓRDOBA

BYZANTINE
EMPIRE

PERSIA

MEDITERRANEAN SEA

BAGHDAD

NORTH AFRICA

Scholars have only recently begun to study interactions between Saami and Norse-speaking Scandinavians at this period. There is good evidence that the two peoples traded with one another. There are also mentions of Saami paying "tribute" to Norse chiefs and traders who used force and other means to exploit them. Some Scandinavians became very wealthy thanks to these payments. As a ninth-century Norwegian merchant named Ottar explained,

> That tribute consists of the skins of the [reindeer] herds, the feathers of birds, whalebone and ship rope made from walrus hide and sealskin. Each pays according to his rank. The highest in rank has to pay fifteen marten skins, five reindeer skins, one bear skin, ten measures of feathers, and a jacket of bear skin or otter skin, and two ship ropes . . . one made from walrus hide, the other from seal.

Ottar took these valuable goods and sailed with them down the coast of Norway, stopping to make sales at market centers along the way and then in Denmark and England, too.

LIFE IN SCANDINAVIA

Farm families made up the majority of the population in the Middle Ages. Norse farmers grew barley, rye, oats, peas, broad beans, cabbage, and onions and other root vegetables. Where the land and climate were right, they also raised flax (which provided both linen and nourishing flaxseeds), hemp (which provided fiber for rope and other uses), hops (which helped flavor beer), herbs, and dye plants such as woad (which gave a blue dye). Only in the warmer, more fertile southern parts of Scandinavia could farmers grow wheat—north of Denmark, wheat bread was usually a luxury.

On farms in very cold, rugged areas, livestock were the main focus,

but they were important on all farms. Cattle were raised for meat, milk, leather, and pulling carts and plows; sheep for wool, meat, milk, and skins; goats for milk and meat; geese and chickens for eggs, feathers, and meat; and horses—the most valuable animals—for pulling vehicles and riding. People sometimes ate horsemeat, too, which may have been part of special religious rites. Pork was also eaten on special occasions, but mostly by the upper class; pigs were not found on the average farm.

Hunting and fishing were important parts of rural life, especially where it was difficult to grow crops or hay for the winter feeding of livestock. And just as people could sell or trade their surplus farm products, they could sell or trade their surplus game, game products (such as furs and reindeer antlers), and fish (which could be dried to be preserved and transported long distances). Scandinavians also hunted whales, walruses, and seals, sometimes leaving home for lengthy periods to pursue these sea animals. In the north, seal and whale meat might be mainstays of the diet. Seabirds, too, were hunted, and not just for

This Norwegian landscape, with mountains rising up on either side of a fjord, was painted by a Swedish artist in the nineteenth century. The scene would have looked much the same during Viking times.

Walrus were difficult to hunt but also extremely profitable, since their tusks were Europe's main source of ivory—a much-valued material—during most of the Middle Ages.

their meat: feathers and down were much valued for stuffing mattresses, pillows, quilts, and even jackets. Falcons, which could be sold for great profit, were also caught; they would be trained to help human hunters.

Norse farms were often small, and so were rural communities—commonly half a dozen families or fewer. Along with outlying pastureland, each family had its own fenced plot surrounding the house. The family included not only parents and children but also, in many cases, grandparents and unmarried aunts and uncles. In a prosperous household there might be a few servants or slaves, too.

A typical home was a longhouse, divided into two or three sections inside; one section was for animals, at least in the winter. In addition there were usually several outbuildings, which included workshops, hay barns, and storehouses. Rural families were resourceful and independent, producing much of what they needed themselves. Women made thread, cloth, clothing, bread, cheese, sausages, beer, and so on. Men crafted such things as tools, hunting weapons, and fishing boats; farmers typically had considerable skill in carpentry and blacksmithing.

There were also specialized craftsmen, for example smiths who made swords and armor, and others who worked in gold, silver, and bronze to create jewelry and similar luxury items. Artisans like these

often lived in towns and trading centers that were under the patronage of kings, nobles, or great landowners. As in other cultures, the upper class made up the smallest segment of society. In eighth- and ninth-century Scandinavia, though, it was not entirely necessary to be born into this class. A man with a reputation for bravery, leadership, and generosity could gain followers and influence. If he also gained sufficient wealth (which allowed him to acquire even more followers and influence), he could become a powerful *jarl*—a chieftain or noble. Occasionally, he might even become king.

Longhouses, built of stone with thatched roofs, nestle together in this reconstruction of a Norse settlement in Sweden.

LEAD-IN TO THE VIKING AGE

Before the modern era, mountains, dense forests, and marshes made land travel in Scandinavia extremely time-consuming, difficult, and sometimes impossible. Rivers, inlets, and other waterways, however, were abundant, and people took full advantage of them from very early times. They were all-season "roads"—even when they froze over in winter, travelers could still use them, thanks to skis, skates, and sleds.

Most settlements were close to the coasts or to water routes leading to the sea. The sea, along with rivers and lakes, naturally provided food and other resources. Moreover, these waters were the major or

A scene from the Bayeux Tapestry, a long embroidered cloth made to commemorate the Norman conquest of England in 1066. The Normans were descendants of Vikings who settled in what is now France. Their shipbuilding methods, shown here, were virtually the same as those in Scandinavia.

only way of linking together widely separated settlements for trade, government, and other purposes. Considering how much Scandinavians depended on the sea and other waterways, it is not surprising that they became expert boatbuilders.

The waters in and around their homelands were largely sheltered from strong winds, so early Scandinavian boats were slim, light, maneuverable, and propelled by paddles—rather like large canoes. By the third century, most likely, oars had come into use. They cut through the waves with greater power and could propel larger boats, some of which were capable of carrying Scandinavians on occasional voyages to other parts of Europe.

Sails probably were not added until the fifth century, and perhaps then just in parts of Denmark. On the Baltic island of Gotland, picture stones from the fifth and sixth centuries show only rowing boats; sailing ships were not portrayed till the seventh century. After that, ships under sail featured in many Gotland picture stones, which have been some of our best sources for the appearance of these vessels and their rigging.

Sails made sense as Scandinavians ventured out of their home waters more frequently. Sailing ships, which could be built bigger than rowing boats, were just the thing for crossing the rough northern seas. In the growing market centers of England and continental Europe, such

Scandinavian products as amber, furs, down, iron, sharpening stones, and walrus ivory were coming into high demand. Scandinavians, in turn, were eager for a variety of southern luxury items, not to mention the silver coins that some European rulers were starting to mint.

It soon became obvious to many Scandinavians that there was a lot of wealth in places like Frankia (modern France, Belgium, Netherlands, and Germany). It also became clear that most coastal towns and monasteries were defenseless. The majority of Europeans believed that they only had to fear attack by land and that being next to the sea helped protect them from enemies. Even if an enemy did come from the sea, most sailors of that era hugged the coastlines, so their ships were usually sighted long before they made an attack, giving plenty of time to prepare a defense. Scandinavian sailors, however, cut directly across the North Sea, so there was little or no warning of their coming. Moreover, their ships were far superior to any vessel most Europeans knew of or could imagine.

Scandinavian ships were sleek and very fast. Their keel design and flexible construction made them extremely stable even in heavy swells. They went under sail at sea, then switched to oars for greater maneuverability close to land. They had such a shallow draft that they could navigate rivers that were only a few feet deep. They could run

A Gotland picture stone shows some of the distinctive features of a Viking ship: the single mast, the large rectangular sail, and the high stem and stern. The men aboard ship are armed in typical Viking fashion, with conical helmets and round shields.

right up onto a beach, then put out to sea again with hardly any delay. And they were crewed by men who knew how to fight as well as how to sail. No wonder that some of those men decided they could make more profit by raiding than trading. Even before the shock of the raid on Lindisfarne in 793, there was at least one other raid in England, and there may have already been some attacks on the islands of northern Scotland.

As the eighth century drew to an end, the temptation of all those wealthy, undefended coastal communities became diffcult to resist—and the Scandinavians had everything they needed to go after these riches. Their land provided a natural abundance of the essential ship-building resources of timber and iron (to make rivets for fastening ship planks in place). Plus, there were plenty of men with the know-how to build and sail the ships, and the ambition to take them on voyages in search of wealth.

The men were motivated, at least in part, by changing conditions in Scandinavia itself. In some areas an increase in population may have been making good farmland scarce. Political struggles were becoming common as Danish kings asserted more authority over local chiefs and also fought to extend their power into the Scandinavian Peninsula. Defeated or out-of-favor leaders and their followers were often forced to leave their homelands. And loot and glory gained abroad gave men power when they returned home. For these reasons and more, Scandinavian raiders became much more active than they had been in past centuries. Historians have given the period of this increased activity, usually dated from 793 to 1066, a handy nickname: the Viking Age.

BUILDING A SHIP

WRITING AROUND 1220, ICELANDIC historian Snorri Sturluson recounted the building of one of the Viking Age's famous ships, which sailed to war in the year 1000 with more than two hundred men aboard:

Long Serpent's sail fills with wind as Norwegian king Olaf Tryggvason leads his fleet to war.

> King Olaf . . . had a great vessel built which was larger than any ship in the country. . . . The keel that rested upon the grass was seventy-four ells [about 120 feet] long. Thorberg Skaffhog was the name of the man in charge of making the stem and stern of the vessel but there were many others, some to fell wood, some to shape it, some to make nails, some to carry timber. All that was used was very carefully chosen. The ship was long and broad and strongly timbered. While they were planking the ship, it happened that Thorberg had to go home to his farm on urgent business and he stayed there a long time. The ship was planked up on both sides when he returned. That same evening the king went out with Thorberg to see how the vessel looked and everybody said that so large and beautiful a ship of war had never been seen before. . . . Thorberg was the master-builder of the ship until she was finished. The ship was a dragon, built like the one the king had captured in Halogaland but this one was much larger and more carefully made in all her parts. The king called this ship *Long Serpent* and the other *Short Serpent*. *Long Serpent* had thirty-four benches for rowers. The prow and the stern were covered in gilding. . . . This ship was the best and most costly one ever built in Norway.

FIGHTING for LOOT and LAND

A MEDIEVAL SAGA, OR TALE, ABOUT NORSE SETTLERS IN THE Orkney Islands (off the northern tip of Scotland) recounted the annual routine of a landowner named Svein Asleifsson, who lived in the 1100s. In springtime,

> he had more than enough to occupy him, with a great deal of seed to sow which he saw to carefully himself. Then when that job was done, he would go off plundering in the Hebrides [a group of islands in western Scotland] and in Ireland on what he called his 'spring-trip'; then back home just after midsummer, where he stayed till the ... fields had been reaped and the grain was safely in. After that he would go off raiding again, and never came back till the first month of winter was ended. This he called his 'autumn-trip'.

Like Svein Asleifsson, the majority of men who sailed out for plunder were not full-time raiders. For most of the year, they occupied

Opposite page: A Viking hero prepares to slay a giant serpent in a carving that adorns the door of the city hall in Oslo, the capital of Norway.

This painting from a twelfth-century English manuscript shows a band of Viking raiders coming ashore in the British Isles. Although the ships are drawn very small and without masts and sails, their shape is accurately portrayed.

themselves with the land and its tasks, and thought of themselves as farmers. Only when they went away on an expedition would they be considered Vikings. The Old Norse phrase *fara i Viking*, usually translated "to go a-viking," basically meant to go off on a voyage for profit. That profit might be obtained through trading or raiding, or a combination of both. But for those who came to know these seafarers primarily as raiders—sometimes within Scandinavia itself—*Viking* became another word for *pirate*.

IRELAND AND THE WESTERN ISLES

A year after the raid on Lindisfarne, Vikings attacked another Northumbrian monastery, Jarrow. The following year, as chroniclers in Wales noted, "the pagans first came to Ireland and Racline [Rathlin, an island monastery] was destroyed." Vikings also sacked at least two other Irish religious communities that season, as well as the highly revered monastery of Iona, off the coast of Scotland.

Monasteries on the coasts and islands of Ireland and western Scotland were the Vikings' main targets for the next thirty or so years. According to Irish chronicles, Iona alone was attacked at least twice more—burned in 802, and sixty-eight monks killed in 806. This last event shook the community so much that many of the monks left the island and established a new monastery in Kells, Ireland, well inland. Many of the inhabitants of monasteries that remained near the sea seem to have lived in a state of constant fear, or at least vigilance. This is certainly the impression we get from a poem jotted down by a ninth-century Irish monk:

> Bitter is the wind tonight,
> White the tresses of the sea;
> I have no fear the Viking hordes
> Will sail the seas on such a night.

A large part of the monks' distress came from the feeling that the Northmen were singling out holy sites—which they may have been, but not for the antireligious reasons Christians thought. The Irish and Scottish monasteries were not only places of worship and learning but also centers of arts, crafts, and trade. Churches were full of objects that were both valuable and portable. In addition, both monasteries and churches often functioned as "safe deposits" where local people stored their riches. To the Vikings, these wealthy, undefended places were such perfect and easy targets that for a long time they saw no reason to try their luck elsewhere.

Their luck, however, did not always hold out. Even early on, they sometimes met with resistance. For example, the *Anglo-Saxon Chronicle* related that during the 794 raid on Jarrow, "one of their leaders was slain, and also some of their ships were wrecked by tempest, and many of them were drowned, and some came to shore alive, and they were there slain at the mouth of the river." Nevertheless, attacking monastic settlements was probably less risky for the Vikings than attacking the well-defended towns of England and Frankia.

BOTH SIDES OF THE CHANNEL

Vikings made a raid in western Frankia in 799, but the Frankish emperor Charlemagne responded immediately and strongly. He estab-

A modern artist imagined this scene of Charlemagne angrily watching from a battlement as Vikings land on the Frankish coast.

lished a coastguard, ordered forts built along the coast, and stationed fleets of ships at the mouths of rivers. But after Charlemagne died in 814, his empire began to fall apart as his heirs fought among themselves more and more.

Soon the Frankish coasts became vulnerable, nowhere more so than in Frisia (today's Netherlands and northwest Germany). Charlemagne's navy no longer existed, and without a navy, the long, low-lying Frisian coastline was impossible to protect. Three times between 834 and 837, Vikings pillaged the great Frisian trading center of Dorestad. A Frankish chronicler wrote of the 834 raid (probably exaggerating somewhat), "The Danes attacked Dorestad and destroyed everything, slaughtered some people, took others away captive, and burned the surrounding region."

Since Denmark was only a short sail from Frisia, the Vikings in this case probably did come from there. The Franks and the English, however, often referred to all Scandinavian raiders as Danes, regardless of where in Scandinavia they actually came from. (The earlier Vikings who harried Ireland and western Scotland were probably from Norway for the most part.) In any case, the Northmen were now turning their ambitions to both sides of the English Channel. The *Anglo-Saxon Chronicle* records renewed Viking activity in England beginning in 835, when "heathen men ravaged [the island of] Sheppey." The next year, the ruler of the southern English kingdom of Wessex "fought with twenty-five ship companies at Carhampton, and there was great slaughter; the Danes held the battlefield."

The Northmen not only carried off valuables but also people, whom they held for ransom or sold into slavery. What they could not take away, they sometimes destroyed. This kind of violence was not at all unusual in early medieval Europe but, to their victims, the Vikings seemed to carry it to a great extreme. The attacks were the more terrifying because of their unexpectedness and lightning swiftness. By the time a Viking ship or fleet was sighted, there was no chance to prepare a defense before the raiders landed. And by the time a counterattack could be launched, the Northmen were already back in their ships, sailing away.

By the middle of the ninth century, few places in western Europe were safe from Viking raids. In 844 a fleet reached Muslim-ruled Iberia and fell upon Lisbon, Cadiz, and Seville before the Arab army stopped their progress. Elsewhere the Northmen were sailing up rivers, striking ever farther inland. They attacked not just villages, monasteries, and small towns, but cities such as London, Paris, and Hamburg.

The Viking attack on Paris in 845 was remembered for hundreds of years, as this illustration, made in 1884, shows.

A Frankish chronicle told how in 845, "the Northmen with a hundred ships entered the Seine on the twentieth of March and, after ravaging first one bank and then the other, came without meeting any resistance to Paris." The king, Charles the Bald, realized he could not defeat them, so paid them 7,000 pounds of silver to leave. They sailed back up the Seine peaceably enough, but "coming to the ocean pillaged, destroyed, and burned all the regions along the coast."

SETTLING IN

In the early decades of the Viking Age, raids were hit-and-run affairs. The Northmen generally went on expeditions only in the summer months and then sailed back to their homes. But in the winter of 842 they broke this pattern in Frankia and established themselves on an island near the mouth of the Loire River. Vikings wintered in England for the first time in 850, on the small island of Thanet in the southeast. From such bases the Northmen continued to head out on raids. For some Scandinavians, year-round raiding was developing into a way of life.

This had also become apparent in Ireland, where Vikings first stayed the winter in 839 or 840. In 841 they established a *longphort*, a fortified landing place for their ships, at Dublin. The next year an Irish chronicler noted, "Pagans still in Dublin"—clearly he had not expected them to stay. But not only did they remain in Dublin, they founded other *longphorts* that became permanent towns. From these they made forays ever deeper into the country. They seemed to be everywhere. A chronicle entry for the year 847 claimed, "After they had been under attack from the Vikings for many years, the Irish were made tributaries to them; the Vikings have possessed themselves without opposition of all the islands round about and have settled on them." In fact, there was opposition: several times during the 800s, Irish kings left off their feuding with one another and fought the Northmen, often succesfully. Nevertheless, Vikings continued to raid and settle through much of Ireland.

The same kind of thing was happening elsewhere. By the middle of the ninth century, Norwegian Vikings were well established in northern Scotland, especially in the Shetland and Orkney Islands. Probably during the same period they were colonizing the Isle of Man in the Irish Sea. Some settlements were also made in southwest Wales. In many cases these Viking colonies in the British Isles were no longer just bases for raids—they also became places where the Norse settled down to farm and raise their families.

PIRATE ISLANDS

"IT IS RELATED THAT IN THE DAYS OF HARALD FINEHAIR [died around 940], THE KING of Norway, the islands of Orkney, which before had been only a resort for Vikings, were settled." This sentence from one of the sagas confirms that Vikings had been using the Scottish islands as a base for some time. And they continued to do so long after they established permanent homes and farms. Another saga relates,

> One summer Harald Finehair sailed west to punish the Vikings, as he had grown tired of their depredations, for they harried in Norway during the summer, but spent the winter in Shetland or the Orkneys. He subdued Shetland and the Orkneys ... he fought there many battles and annexed the land farther west than any Norwegian king has done since.

Coming under control of the Norwegian crown may have stopped the Shetland and Orkney Islanders from raiding in Norway, but it didn't keep them from sailing south to prey on other targets. The Orkneyman we met on p. 23, Svein Asleifsson, was still at it in the twelfth century, leading a band of eighty warriors in seasonal raids on Ireland, Wales, and the Hebrides Islands. In 1171 he even took part in an effort to capture Dublin. It was his last adventure: the attempt failed, and Svein was killed in the fighting.

Above: *King Harald Finehair with a Viking leader named Guthrum, from a fourteenth-century Icelandic manuscript*

ARMIES OF CONQUEST

In 866 a new chapter opened in the story of the Vikings. That year, said the *Anglo-Saxon Chronicle*, "a great heathen force came into English land, and they took winter-quarters in East Anglia." This force has become known as the Great Army, although it was not really the kind of organized body we think of as an army. It probably numbered a few thousand men, mostly from Denmark, under a number of different leaders. In 867 they besieged and captured York, the capital of Northumbria. The kingdoms of East Anglia and Mercia fell to the Great Army in the 870s. Only Wessex, England's southernmost kingdom, was able to resist, thanks to the leadership (and good luck) of its king, Alfred the Great.

A twentieth-century mural in the Houses of Parliament in London shows King Alfred's forces fighting the Danes.

For a decade the Great Army roamed England during the summers, fighting and looting along the way, and spent the winters in various fortified camps. But in 876 one of the commanders, Halfdan, divided Northumbria among his men, who settled down to farm—"they were ploughing and providing for themselves," says the *Anglo-Saxon Chronicle*. In the next few years Mercia and East Anglia were shared out to other divisions of the Great Army. In a treaty of 886, Alfred the Great formally ceded most of Northumbria, half of Mercia, and all of East Anglia to the Vikings.

The sizeable portion of eastern and northern England under Viking control became known as the Danelaw. Its raiders-turned-farmers were soon joined by new Scandinavian immigrants. The Danelaw's greatest center was York, which became the capital of the Kingdom of York. The city, located on England's major north-south land route, attracted merchants from all over the Viking world. Crafts and trade flourished, and by 1000 York was the second-largest city in England (after London), with a population nearing 10,000.

In 902 Alfred the Great's son and successor, Edward, began to conquer the Danelaw. That same year the Norwegian Vikings of Dublin were driven out of Ireland, and many of them migrated to York. They returned to Ireland beginning in 915 and refounded Dublin and other bases, which developed into thriving trading centers. A number of these still exist today as important Irish cities, including Limerick, Waterford, Wexford, and Cork.

Back in England, in 917 Edward and his sister Aethelflaed, queen of Mercia, decisively defeated the Scandinavians of the Danelaw. By the next year the Danes controlled only the Kingdom of York. Its king had planned to surrender to Aethelflaed, but she died before that could happen. Instead Rognvald, the Norwegian ruler of Dublin, took over York in 919. During the next decades the kingdom changed hands several times; the last Viking king of York was the Norwegian Erik Bloodaxe, killed in battle in 954.

VIKING WOMEN

WHEN A SCANDINAVIAN MAN WENT OFF A-VIKING, HE DIDN'T HAVE TO WORRY ABOUT leaving his farm—at least if he was married. His wife would both run and protect the farm in his absence. Viking Age women were expected to be as strong, brave, and resourceful as men. But while a man could earn honor and respect by gaining wealth and doing great deeds abroad, a woman earned honor and respect by wisely using and guarding that wealth at home. It was she who carried the keys for the family's storerooms and storage chests.

Sometimes, though, women did go abroad with their menfolk. There is little evidence of women participating in raids, but plenty of evidence of their presence on other Viking voyages. A great many Scandinavian women left their homelands to settle in Viking colonies. Most of these women emigrated with their husbands, but there were also widows who settled independently. In addition, we know that Scandinavian merchants sometimes traveled with their wives, and it is possible that some traveling women were merchants in their own right.

Even when women didn't go a-viking themselves, they made it possible for others to do so, and not just by tending the home fires while the men were away. Spinning and weaving cloth was women's work, so it was women who made the woolen sails for Viking ships. One scholar has estimated that the sail of a Viking warship required more than 930 square feet of cloth—enough fabric to make clothes for forty people. That's a lot of spinning and weaving!

Above: Viking women were expected to be strong and brave. A modern Russian artist imagines an ideal Viking princess in this portrait.

Many members of the Great Army had chosen not to settle in England but went on to raid Frankia. "The number of ships grows," wrote the monk Ermentarius around 860. "The endless stream of Vikings never ceases to increase. Everywhere the Christians are the victims of massacres, burnings, plunderings: the Vikings conquer all in their path, and no one resists them . . . and an innumerable fleet sails up the Seine and the evil grows in the whole region." Ermentarius listed cities throughout what is now France that had been "laid waste"—besieged, plundered, captured, and/or burned.

In 911 the Frankish king Charles the Simple granted land around Rouen, near the mouth of the Seine River, to a Viking leader known as Rollo. In exchange, Rollo agreed to defend northern Frankia from other Vikings, and for several years he and his men did so. Then Rollo began leading raids on Frankish territory himself. He greatly extended the region under his control, and his son continued this process. The area settled by Rollo's Northmen was named Normandy after them. Rollo's descendants, who became Christians, ruled as the dukes of Normandy for generations afterward.

Rollo, shown here dressed as a French knight, was also known as Hrolf the Walker. He got his nickname, it was said, because he was too large for any horse to carry, so he had to walk everywhere.

In 914 Rollo also helped a large Viking army conquer Brittany (now, like Normandy, part of France). But the Norwegians in Brittany never settled down to farm or trade. They simply continued to plunder the region until the Bretons at last drove them out in 939. That was the end of large-scale Viking activity in Frankia, although isolated raids occurred into the eleventh century. Meanwhile, Viking energies found outlets on the familiar coasts around the Irish Sea, and also in unfamiliar and far-off places to both west and east.

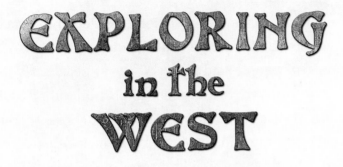

EXPLORING in the WEST

OTTAR, THE MERCHANT WE MET ON PAGE 14, VISITED THE court of Alfred the Great in the 880s and, at the king's request, described his homeland: "He said that the land of the Norwegians was very long and very narrow. All that they can either graze or plough lies by the sea; and even that is very rocky in some places; and to the east, and alongside the cultivated land, lie wild mountains." No wonder, then, that Norwegians wanting more farmland looked to the west, across the sea. And from southern Norway, given good weather, it would take only twenty-four hours of sailing to reach the Shetland Islands. South of these were the Orkneys, and then mainland Scotland. As we have already seen, Northmen were quite familiar with these areas by the early ninth century.

Soon, though, there were rumors of even more lands in the sea to the west. Around 825 an Irish monk named Dicuil wrote of a "set of small islands, nearly all separated by narrow stretches of water; in these for nearly a hundred years hermits sailing from our country, Ireland,

Opposite page: Vikings explore the seas in a quest for more land.

35

have lived. But . . . now because of the Northman pirates they are emptied of anchorites [hermits], and are filled with countless sheep and very many diverse kinds of seabirds." Indeed, the Norwegian Vikings who settled these islands in the ninth century named them the Faeroes—"sheep islands."

According to the sagas, the first Norse settler in the Faeroes was a man named Grim Kamban. Then, "in the days of King Harald Finehair a great number of people fled [from Norway] because of his tyranny. Some settled in the Faeroes and made their home there, while others went to other uninhabited countries." King Harald's efforts to bring all of Norway under his rule did in fact threaten the independence and land rights of many chieftains, no doubt inspiring a number of them to emigrate. But colonization of the "uninhabited countries" was probably under way at least ten years before Harald's reign began in the 870s.

ICELAND

The discovery and settlement of Iceland were recorded in histories and sagas composed in the twelfth and thirteenth centuries. These tales were sometimes highly embellished, but they were often based on local traditions and memories handed down through the descendants of the founding families. They told how the first Scandinavians to find their way to Iceland were a Norwegian, Naddod, followed by a Swede, Gardar Svafarsson. Neither man attempted to settle the land they'd found, but word of their voyages spread.

Around 860, Floki Vilgerdarson left Norway planning not only to explore the North Atlantic island but to settle on it. He stopped at the Shetlands and Faeroes along the way, then headed northwest. With him he brought three ravens, birds sacred to the god Odin. Not knowing how long or far he was supposed to sail, he released the first raven, which flew back toward the Faeroes. After going farther, he released the second bird, which circled overhead and then returned to the ship. Floki sailed on. Then he let loose the third raven, and it flew straight ahead to the horizon. Floki followed, and at last sighted land.

He and his men beached their ship in an inlet. The history relates,

> The fjord teemed with fish of all kinds, and they were so busy fishing that they paid no heed to gathering hay for the winter; and that winter, all their livestock died. The following spring was an extremely cold one. Flóki climbed a high mountain and looked north towards the coast, and saw a fjord choked with drift-ice; and so they called the country *Ísland* [Iceland], and that has been its name ever since.

Iceland had plenty of free land, but many other resources were limited. The wood for this panel (part of a scene of Jesus with Christian saints, carved in the 1000s or 1100s) had to be imported from Norway.

A year later Floki returned to Norway, convinced that Iceland was not worth settling. But a couple of his men thought otherwise. One was careful to describe both the good points and bad points of the island. The other was so enthusiastic about Iceland's advantages that he claimed "butter dripped from every blade of grass."

One sure advantage was that Iceland had no human inhabitants, so the land was free for the taking. This was enough of a lure to persuade many people to gather their families and livestock, pack up their most important possessions, and attempt the potentially dangerous ocean crossing. The sagas say that the first successful settlers were two men named Ingolf and Hjorleif, who had lost their lands in Norway when they had to pay compensation for murders they'd committed.

AUD THE DEEP-MINDED

ONE OF ICELAND'S MOST PROMINENT SETTLERS WAS AUD THE DEEP-MINDED, whose father had been the Norse ruler of the Hebrides. After her husband, a Norse king of Dublin, was killed, she returned to the Hebrides. From there her son Thorstein conquered northern Scotland, and she went to live in his new domain. Then "the Scots betrayed him, and he fell there in battle." Upon learning of her son's death, Aud "caused a merchant ship to be made in a wood, in secret, and when it was ready she held out to the Orkneys; there she gave in marriage Gro, the daughter of Thorstein." Next she stopped in the Faeroes, where she arranged the marriage of another of Thorstein's daughters. Afterward she headed for Iceland, where two of her brothers were already settled. She stayed with one brother for the winter, then "went to seek a settlement . . . accompanied by her liegemen." They traveled by ship, of course, and after a day or so of sailing, she

selected an extensive territory along a bay in western Iceland. But she did not keep all this land for herself: "Aud gave lands to her shipmates and freed-men." After settling her followers, she proceeded to arrange marriages for Thorstein's remaining daughters. The *Book of Settlements*, which tells of these events, praises Aud as "a great lady of state." It continues, "when she was weary with old age," she invited her friends, followers, and extensive family to "a most stately feast; and whenas the feast had stood for three nights, she bestowed gifts upon her friends, and gave them wholesome counsels. . . . The next night she died, and was buried on the shore."

Above: After the deaths of her husband and son, Aud the Deep-Minded took charge of her family's fortunes, sailing from Scotland to the Orkneys to the Faeroe Islands and, finally, to Iceland.

Upon arrival, Hjorleif immediately chose a site on the southern coast. Ingolf, on the other hand, tossed the wooden pillars that supported his high seat into the waves, trusting that the gods would use them to lead him to a good place. It was said that it took him nearly three years to find where the pillars had washed ashore. When he did, he built his home there, near the site of Reykjavik, modern Iceland's capital. Hjorleif, however, met an unhappy end, murdered by his slaves.

These slaves were people Hjorleif had captured during raids on Ireland. There were quite a few Irish and Scottish slaves among Iceland's early settlers. The Scandinavian colonists were mostly from western Norway, but there were also Danes, Swedes, and Saami. Some of these settlers came direct from Scandinavia, while others emigrated from the Norse colonies in Scotland and Ireland. A number of the Vikings expelled from Dublin in 902 decided to try their luck in Iceland instead of York.

By 930 some twenty thousand people lived in Iceland, farming and raising livestock on the fertile lands of the coasts and river valleys. In this year the island's leading chieftains established the Althing, a kind of national assembly that met for two weeks every June. From all over Iceland, people came to the plain of Thingvellir, where an elected official known as the Lawspeaker proclaimed the laws. Courts met to settle quarrels and feuds—by negotiation if possible, but by punishments such as exile if necessary. The Althing was also a great social occasion, with far-flung family members reuniting, young people court-

A meeting of Iceland's Althing, with the Lawspeaker presiding from the rock at the center. The artist, W. G. Collingwood, researched the painting's details during a trip to Iceland in the 1870s.

ing, peddlers and merchants selling their wares, and travelers sharing news of their voyages.

GREENLAND

Around 980 a hot-tempered settler named Erik the Red was convicted of manslaughter and banished from Iceland for three years. Erik had heard tales of some new land to the west and decided to find it and spend his exile there. So it was that Erik came to the huge island he named Greenland. When he returned to Iceland in 986 he recruited twenty-five shiploads of settlers to join him in colonizing the new land. "Fourteen reached it, some were driven back [to Iceland] and some were lost."

That brief statement from the Icelandic *Book of Settlements* highlights the risks of these oversea voyages. The dangers included storms, high waves, whirlpools, and floating sea ice. Unfavorable winds

Erik the Red aboard his ship. His helmet is pure fantasy, but his sword, clothes, beard, and mustache are close to styles seen in Viking Age art and artifacts.

could double or triple a journey's length or blow a ship completely off course. Even when sailing close to land—which Norse navigators tried to do whenever possible—there were hazards for ships, such as fog and darkness that hid rocky coasts or outcrops. Viking Age travelers usually tried to avoid night sailing for this reason.

NORSE SAILORS DID NOT HAVE COMPASSES OR OTHER SOPHISTICATED INSTRUMENTS TO guide them on their voyages. They mainly relied on things like their knowledge of weather patterns, animal behavior, and landmarks. Such information was passed on from sailor to sailor, down the generations. A thirteenth-century Icelandic manuscript preserved some traditional directions for navigating the North Atlantic. Although most of the place-names may be unfamiliar, this is an interesting example of how the Norse found their way across the sea and of how long it took them to get from one land to another, at least when the winds were right and the seas were calm.

SAILING TIMES AND GUIDELINES

Wise men say that from Stad in Norway it is seven days' sailing to Horn in eastern Iceland, but from Snaefellsnes [a peninsula in western Iceland] it is four days' sailing to Hvarf in Greenland. From Hernar in Norway one should keep sailing west to reach Hvarf in Greenland and then you are sailing north of Shetland, so that it can only be seen if visibility is very good, but south of the Faeroes, so that the sea appears half-way up their mountain slopes, but so far south of Iceland that one is only aware of birds and whales from it. From Reykjanes in southern Iceland it is three days' sailing south to Slyne Head in Ireland; but from Langanes in northern Iceland it is four days' sailing north to Svalbardi at the end of the ocean, but a day's sailing to the wastes of Greenland from Kolbeinsey [an island north of Iceland] to the north.

Above: A silver coin minted around 825 in Hedeby, Denmark, depicts a cargo ship with its sail furled.

A peaceful voyage that went exactly as planned still had its share of hardships. Settlers sailed in a type of cargo ship called a knorr. Knorrs were broader, deeper, and sturdier than the fast, sleek longships used in Viking raids. But every bit of space in the knorr would be crammed full with the livestock and possessions of the ship's crew and their families. Only cold food could be eaten during the journey, since cooking posed too great a risk of fire. The sole shelter from the elements may have been a rough tent. There was no privacy, and no place to go to the bathroom except over the ship's side. The farm animals wouldn't even bother with that, and they were even more likely to get seasick than the human passengers were.

Once the settlers reached their destination, hardships continued. Timber was not abundant in the North Atlantic colonies, where most of the trees (if any) were small birches and willows. Houses were generally built from stone or blocks of turf, and tools often had to be made from driftwood or bone. Wood for shipbuilding had to be imported. Some North Atlantic islands also lacked other natural resources that Scandinavians traditionally depended on, such as iron and soapstone (commonly used to make cooking pots, fishing sinkers, and other useful items). The colonies relied on trade with mainland Europe for many of their needs.

Unlike in the Faeroes and Iceland, it was impossible to grow grain and other food crops in Greenland, even in the warmest, most sheltered areas. These places did offer good pastureland for livestock, however. The Greenlanders were also able to raise hay so that they could feed their animals during the winter. In addition, Greenlanders hunted caribou, birds, and sea animals for food and for resources such as bone, antler, oil, and furs. Moreover, many made seasonal hunting trips to the island's freezing northwest coast to procure walrus ivory, polar bear skins, and other animal products that brought high prices in Europe. Trading in such luxury items was essential since Greenlanders, even more than other Scandinavian colonists in the North Atlantic, depended heavily on imports.

Despite all the challenges, Erik the Red and his companions, and their descendants after them, built good lives for themselves. Eventually there were three settlements, home to a population of at least a couple thousand people. As for Erik, the former outlaw became Greenland's leading citizen. He also passed his resourcefulness and spirit of adventure on to his children, who made some of the world's most historic voyages of exploration.

A NEW WORLD

In 986 an off-course Icelandic merchant named Bjarni Herjolfsson happened upon lands even farther to the west than Greenland. Because he wanted to get to Greenland as quickly as possible (his parents had unexpectedly immigrated there

while he was off on a trading voyage), he never went ashore. He did, however, tell some of the Greenlanders about the lands he had sighted. Around the year 1000, Erik the Red's son Leif set out to find them.

This twelfth-century chess piece came from one of the Norse-ruled Hebrides Islands. It was crafted from walrus ivory, one of Greenland's most valuable exports.

Leif's nickname was "the Lucky," and he certainly had good fortune as an explorer. He found what he was looking for, and he became (as far as we know) the first European to set foot in North America. He and his crew explored a region he named Vinland, which most scholars believe was in southeastern Canada. After spending the winter there, the Greenlanders returned home.

Then, says the saga, "There was great discussion of Leif's Vinland voyage and his brother Thorvald felt they had not explored enough of the land." Thorvald therefore led thirty men to Leif's Vinland base, Leifsbudir, and they spent two summers in further exploration.

A reconstructed Viking longhouse at L'Anse aux Meadows. Based on archaeologists' discoveries, it was built almost entirely with squares of turf. In Viking times the wooden parts, such as the door frames, were probably made from driftwood.

Although Leif and his men had not encountered any of the natives of North America, Thorvald and his party did. Unfortunately violence broke out, and there were deaths on both sides; Thorvald was one of those killed.

The next summer, Icelandic merchant Thorfinn Karlsefni arrived at Erik the Red's farm. There he married Gudrid, the widow of Erik's son Thorstein (who had also sailed for Vinland at one point, but had been unable to reach it). Gudrid and Thorfinn decided to continue the explorations. Thorfinn "hired himself a crew of sixty men and five women. . . . Then they put out to sea and arrived without mishap at Leifsbudir."

After a time they established a base named Straumfjord, from which they could strike out to explore the land further and trade with its natives. Some scholars believe that Straumfjord was at the place now known as L'Anse aux Meadows in Newfoundland. In any case, archaeologists have found plenty of evidence that L'Anse aux Meadows was a substantial Viking base where as many as ninety people could have lived. The finds have given other valuable information, too. For example, iron rivets show that ships were repaired here, while a soapstone spindle whorl (part of the equipment for spinning wool) shows that women were part of this community, just as the sagas say.

At first Gudrid and Thorfinn's party traded peaceably with the area's Native Americans. But before long the explorers were fighting with the natives as well as quarreling among themselves. After two winters they decided to return to Greenland, "taking with them plenty of the land's products," which included wood, furs, and dried grapes or berries. There was also a new member of their party: Gudrid and Thorfinn's son Snorri, the first European child born in North America.

"Discussion soon began again of a Vinland voyage, since the trip seemed to bring men both wealth and renown." The leader of the new venture was Leif's sister Freydis, who invited two Norwegian men to join her. However, their ship reached Vinland before hers did, and they tried to take over Leifsbudir. Even after that situation was resolved, hostilities between Freydis and the Norwegians only increased. The conflict became so bad during the winter that Freydis had her men kill the Norwegian men, and she herself killed the women who had sailed with them. Freydis returned successfully to Greenland in the spring, her ship loaded with the produce of Vinland.

This is how the story of Freydis goes in one of the sagas. In the other surviving version of her deeds, Freydis is a heroine, defending her fellow explorers against an attack by Native Americans. But whatever the truth may have been, the sagas tell of no further Norse explorations of Vinland after her voyage. Nevertheless, other texts, along with archaeological finds, make it clear that Greenlanders continued to travel to North America for timber, iron, and other resources well into the fourteenth century. After that, however, the Greenland colonies died out, and there was no further Norse contact with the New World.

An inside view of the L'Anse aux Meadows longhouse. People worked, ate, and slept on the raised platform along the side. A central hearth provided light and heat.

GREENLANDERS' SAGA, PRESERVED IN A SINGLE FOURTEENTH-CENTURY MANUSCRIPT, is one of our earliest records of European exploration in North America. Here is the story of Leif Eriksson's remarkable journey:

There was now much talk [in Greenland] of looking for new lands. Leif . . . sought out Bjarni and purchased his ship. He hired himself a crew numbering thirty-five men. . . .

Once they had made the ship ready they put to sea and found first the land which Bjarni and his companions had seen last. They sailed up to the shore and cast anchor, put out a boat and rowed ashore. There they found no grass, but large glaciers covered the highlands and the land was like a single flat slab of rock from the glaciers to the sea. This land seemed to them of little use. Leif then spoke: "As far as this land is concerned it can't be said of us as of Bjarni that we did not set foot on shore. I am now going to name this land and call it Helluland [stone-slab land]."

THE VOYAGE OF LEIF THE LUCKY

They then returned to their ship, put out to sea and found a second land. Once more they sailed close to the shore and cast anchor, put out a boat and

Above: *Leif Eriksson, manning his ship's steering oar, sights the North American coast, as imagined by Norwegian artist Christian Krohg.*

went ashore. This land was flat and forested, sloping gently seaward, and they came across many beaches of white sand. Leif then spoke: "This land shall be named for what it has to offer and called Markland [forest land]." . . .

After this they sailed out to sea and spent two days at sea with a northeasterly wind before they saw land. They sailed toward it and came to an island, which lay to the north of the land, where they went ashore. In the fine weather they found dew on the grass, which they collected in their hands and drank of, and thought they had never tasted anything as sweet.

Afterwards they returned to their ship. . . . They rounded the headland and steered westward. . . . Their curiosity to see the land was so great that they . . . ran ashore where a river flowed into the sea from a lake. . . . They carried their sleeping sacks ashore and built booths. Later they decided to spend the winter there and built large houses.

There was no lack of salmon both in the lake and the river, and this salmon was larger than they had ever seen before. It seemed to them the land was good, that the livestock would need no fodder during the winter. The temperature never dropped below freezing and the grass only withered very slightly. . . .

When they finished building their houses, Leif spoke to his companions: "I want to divide our company into two groups, as I want to explore the land. One half is to remain at home by the longhouses while the other half explores. . . ." This they did for some time. Leif accompanied them sometimes, and at other times remained at home by the houses. Leif was a large, strong man, of very striking appearance and wise, as well as being a man of moderation in all things.

One evening it happened that one man, Tyrker [the German], was missing from their company. . . . [Tyrker returned and] he spoke in Norse: "I had gone only a bit farther than the rest of you. But I have news to tell you; I found grapevines and grapes . . . [I am sure because] where I was born there was no lack of grapevines and grapes. . . ."

When spring came they made the ship ready and set sail. Leif named the land for its natural features and called it Vinland [wineland]. They headed out to sea and had favorable winds, until they came in sight of Greenland.

Salmon were part of the natural abundance that inspired Leif Eriksson and other Greenlanders to consider colonizing North America.

TRADING and RAIDING in the EAST

4

IN 859 TWO VIKINGS NAMED BJORN IRONSIDE AND HASTEIN LED a fleet of sixty-two ships south from western Frankia, around Iberia, and into the Mediterranean. A Frankish chronicler summarized their further exploits: "The Danish pirates having made a long sea-voyage (for they had sailed between Spain and Africa) entered the Rhône, where they pillaged many cities and monasteries and established themselves on the island called Camargue. . . . Thence they went on toward Italy, capturing and plundering Pisa and other cities." Bjorn and Hastein may have continued south after that, and then possibly ventured into the eastern Mediterranean. Eventually, however, they headed back to Frankia, having raided some more in Spain and even in North Africa on the way. Although only twenty ships returned from the three-year adventure, it made Bjorn and Hastein rich and famous. Their voyage had been the most ambitious Viking expedition up to that time. But already, the quest for wealth and glory was taking other Scandinavians even farther to the east.

Opposite page: This painting is an example of the common portrayal of Vikings as bloodthirsty barbarians. It is wrong in nearly all its details, from the chunky ships to the horned helmets, but it does give us a sense of the imprint the Vikings have left on the popular imagination.

49

Swedes in Russia

While Danish and Norwegian Vikings were raiding and settling in western Europe and the North Atlantic, the Vikings of Sweden directed their energies mainly eastward to the lands that now make up Poland, Lithuania, Latvia, Estonia, Finland, Russia, and Ukraine. In these areas they were usually known as the Rus. This term may have come from a word that meant "a crew of oarsmen," which was also the basis of a Finnish name for the Swedes, Ruotsi.

The Rus were warrior-merchants. They went east to trade furs, hides, down, walrus ivory, amber, honey, beeswax, falcons, and slaves for silk, wine, fruit, spices, jewelry, glassware, and, above all, silver coins from the Arab empire based in Baghdad. The empire's merchants were widely traveled, and their currency was in use throughout the east. More than 100,000 Arab coins have been found in hoards buried in Sweden. This is probably just a small fraction of the coinage acquired from the Islamic world, though, since Scandinavians typically melted the silver down and used it to make neck rings, arm rings, and other jewelry—wearable wealth.

Scandinavian and Slavic traders barter goods at a seasonal marketplace.

Rus warrior-merchants portage, or carry their boat overland. Portaging was the best way to travel between waterways.

From trade centers such as the Swedish town of Birka and the island of Gotland, the Rus crossed the Baltic Sea, then followed one of several routes into eastern Europe. On these routes they sailed lakes and rivers and, where necessary, hauled their boats overland to get from one river to the next. One of the first stops was Staraya Ladoga, home to Scandinavian, Finnish, and Slavic craftspeople and merchants since around 750. Here the Rus could acquire, sell, or warehouse goods; have boats built or repaired; and hire guides to help them get through river rapids to the south. Following the river from Staraya Ladoga would lead the Rus to an even richer and more important town, Novgorod. Then the river route continued south to another major center, Kiev on the Dnieper River.

The early years of Novgorod and Kiev were surrounded by legend, as related in an early Russian chronicle:

There arose strife amongst [the Slavic tribes] and they began to fight amongst themselves. And they said to themselves, "Let us find a king to rule over us and make judgements according to

the law." And they crossed the sea. . . . And to the Rus [they] said, "Our land is large and rich, but there is no order in it. So come and be king and rule over us." And three brothers with their kinsfolk were chosen. . . . The eldest, Rurik, settled in Novgorod. . . . And from these [Rus] the Russian land got its name.

The chronicle went on to say that after Rurik died, his successor Oleg (the Slavic form of the Norse name Helgi) captured Kiev from two other Rus leaders around 880. He then "set himself up as prince of Kiev, and declared that it should be the mother of Russian cities."

Archaeological finds have shown that in the ninth century, Scandinavian warriors and merchants made up an elite population in Novgorod,

According to legend, the Slavs invited Rurik to be their king and rule over them.

Kiev, and other centers. Although these Scandinavians were not a majority, they appear to have been in control. Under their influence, the Russian settlements they used as trading bases became thriving, wealthy cities.

Many Rus merchants passed through these centers, making only brief stops before going on to the next destination. Others would live and trade in a town for part of the year and spend the rest of the year at home in Sweden. Still others brought their families and made Staraya

Ladoga, Novgorod, Kiev, or some other town their permanent home. But even when they settled down, their lives were not entirely peaceable. The city-based warrior-merchants exercised power over the people of the surrounding countryside and collected tribute from them, if necessary by force. The tribute was made up of furs and similar goods that the Rus could then trade for other goods or for silver. Many Rus also raided the countryside for slaves, since they made some of their largest profits as slave dealers.

THE GREAT CITY

Every June, Rus merchants gathered in Kiev, waiting for the Dnieper to settle down after the spring floods. Then, joining together in a large fleet for mutual protection, they set sail down the river. In most places the Dnieper was wide and smooth, but on its lower reach there was a series of perilous rapids. Sometimes the merchants tried to steer through them, guided by crewmen who stripped off their clothes, got into the water, and felt their way over the rocks with their bare feet. This was no doubt a dangerous procedure, and there were times when it could not even be attempted. Then the Rus took their ships out of the water and moved them overland on wooden rollers (cut from the nearby forest as needed) till they reached the next stretch of smooth water. But this, too, was dangerous, because local raiders often lay hidden in the woods, waiting to attack when the Rus were most vulnerable.

If all went well, the ships finally came to the Black Sea and sailed across to their goal: the splendid, sprawling city of Constantinople, capital of the Byzantine Empire. Scandinavians knew it simply as Miklagardr, "Great City." Here the Rus found throngs of buyers for their slaves and northern products; markets full of choice goods from all around the eastern Mediterranean and even from distant parts of Asia; and plenty of silver.

Occasionally, however, the Rus were not content with what they could trade for in Constantinople's markets. Around 860 they brought a large fleet to pillage the city and surrounding areas. They stayed for ten days. Raids occurred again in 907 (reportedly led by Oleg of Kiev), 941, and 944. To secure peace, the Byzantines made a series of treaties with the Rus, who agreed not to set up a base at the mouth of the Dnieper, not to bring weapons into the city, not to enter the city without an official escort or written permission—in general, not to cause trouble for the Byzantines. In return, the Rus received easy access to supplies, special trading privileges, and free food, lodgings, and baths. The emperor also made formal arrangements for recruiting Scandinavian warriors to fight in his armies.

Byzantine emperors had been hiring Swedish mercenaries since at least the 830s. In 988 the emperor established an elite, largely Scandinavian unit called the Varangian Guard. The name may come from the Old Norse word meaning "oath" or "vow." As the eleventh-century

The Byzantine emperor visits one of Constantinople's churches, well protected by the members of the Varangian Guard riding behind him.

Byzantine historian Anna Comnena (daughter of one emperor and sister of another) wrote, "They regard loyalty to the emperors . . . as a family tradition, a kind of sacred trust. . . ; this allegiance they preserve inviolate and will never brook the slightest hint of betrayal."

Serving in the Varangian Guard was a good way for men to make their reputation and their fortune. The pay was high and often supplemented by war booty and rich gifts from the emperor. Plus, the prestige of having fought for the emperor of the Great City was bound to enhance a man's status when he returned to Scandinavia. Not surprisingly, Icelanders, Danes, and Norwegians were soon eager to join the Swedes as Varangian recruits. One of the Norwegians even acquired enough wealth and renown during his nine-year service to pave his way to the throne: three years after his return from Constantinople, he became King Harald Hardradi of Norway.

FARTHER EAST

While many Rus went south soon after crossing the Baltic from Sweden, others continued eastward to reach the upper Volga. They had learned that this river would lead them to the very source of Arab silver. They sailed the Volga River to its outlet in the Caspian Sea, then traded along its shores. Some Rus may also have unloaded their ships and switched to camel caravans to travel through northern Persia. We are not certain, but Rus could even have reached the capital of the Islamic world, Baghdad—a city far more wealthy and impressive than Constantinople. Usually the Rus were content just to trade in the strongly defended Arab lands, but there was occasional raiding. For instance, while sailing the Caspian in 912, some Rus attacked Baku and other shoreline communities.

In the tenth century it became rare for the Rus to go so far south. The rulers of Baghdad had been expanding their trade and working out agreements with peoples north of the Caspian Sea. As a result, there

Rurik and his brothers in a 1986 painting by Russian artist Ilya Glazunov. The helmets and jewelry are modeled on finds from Sweden. Viking Age wood carvings show men with neatly combed and trimmed beards and mustaches like Rurik wears here.

were now great trading centers along the Volga where Arab merchants came to do business. So, therefore, did the Rus. One of these cities was Bulgar, the end of a route along which silk was brought from China, and therefore a bustling meeting place of traders and travelers from many places and cultures.

It was while on the way to Bulgar that Ibn Fadlan, a member of a diplomatic mission out of Baghdad, encountered Rus along the Volga in 922. He observed their appearance closely:

I have never seen more perfect physical specimens, tall as date palms, blond and ruddy. . . . Each man has an axe, a sword, and a knife and keeps each by him at all times. . . . Every man is tattooed from finger nails to neck with dark green (or green or blue-black) trees, figures, etc.

Each woman wears [above] either breast a box [brooch] of iron, silver, copper, or gold; the value of the box indicates the wealth of the husband. Each box has a ring from which depends a knife. The women wear neck rings of gold and silver, one for each 10,000 dirhems, which her husband is worth; some women have many. Their most prized ornaments are green glass beads. . . . They string them for necklaces. . . .

Ibn Fadlan also had the opportunity to attend a Rus funeral. The dead man was placed in a ship, which his followers then set on fire. Through an interpreter, one of the Rus explained the reason for this: "You take the people who are most dear to you and whom you honor most and you put them in the ground where insects and worms devour them. We burn him in a moment, so that he enters Paradise at once."

The supply of Arabic silver appears to have dried up toward the end of the tenth century, and so did most Rus trade with the Islamic world. But there was at least one more great journey to the east. In 1036 a twenty-five-year-old warrior named Ingvar set out from Sweden, leading a small fleet along the old route down the Dnieper and into the Black Sea. From there Ingvar and his men seem to have followed another river east to the Caspian Sea and sailed across it. Then, as far as we can tell, they struck out overland, still heading eastward. We don't know where exactly they were heading—perhaps they were trying to find a route to China?

All we know for certain is that the expedition was a disaster in which nearly everybody died. Some thirty stones set up in central Sweden in memory of Ingvar's dead followers testify to this. But the stones give us only hints of what happened out in Serkland (a Norse name for the Islamic east). Later a saga was written about Ingvar the Far-Traveled, a tale of fantastic adventures full of monsters and beautiful princesses. But a memorial-stone inscription tells the true story of the risks of a Viking's life: "Tola had this stone set up in memory of her son, Harald, the brother of Ingvar. With manly prowess they travelled afar for gold. In the east they gave the eagle food [they killed men, leaving their bodies for scavengers]. They died south in Serkland."

ARABS AND SCANDINAVIANS

IBN FADLAN HAS LEFT US ONE OF THE MOST DETAILED EYEWITNESS REPORTS about Viking customs. He even observed a Rus merchant at prayer before "a long upright piece of wood that has a face like a man's and is surrounded by little figures." The man bowed down before the carving and said, "O my Lord, I have come from a far land," named all the things he had brought to sell, then laid out offerings of bread, meat, onions, and milk. He concluded with the appeal, "I want you to send me a merchant who has lots of . . . dirhems and will buy on my terms without being difficult." When business went well, the merchant returned to the carving to give thanks. "Then he takes a certain number of sheep or cattle and kills them. Part of the meat is given away to the poor. The rest is thrown to the tall figure and the smaller figures standing around it."

Above: *Rus warrior-merchants gather at a Slavic settlement along the Dnieper River.*

Other Arab writers recorded additional intriguing observations. A geographer named Ibn Rustah, writing about the same time as Ibn Fadlan, left this description of the Rus in Kiev or Novgorod:

> They fight with the Slavs and use ships to attack them; they take them captive and . . . sell them as slaves. . . . They have no villages, estates or fields. Their only occupation is trading in sable and squirrel and other kinds of skins, which they sell to those who will buy from them. They take coins as payment and fasten them into their belts. They are clean in their clothing, and the men adorn themselves with gold arm-rings. . . . They have many towns. They are generous with their possessions, treat guests honourably, and act handsomely towards strangers who take refuge with them, and all those who accept their hospitality.

Around 950 Ibrahim al-Tartushi, an Arab-Jewish merchant from Iberia, visited Scandinavia itself and had this to say about the town of Hedeby, Denmark:

> They hold a feast where all meet to honour their deity and to eat and drink. Each man who slaughters a sacrificial animal—an ox, ram, goat, or pig—fastens it up on poles outside the door of his house to show that he has made his sacrifice in honour of the god. The town is poorly provided with property or treasure. The inhabitants' principal food is fish, which is very plentiful. The people often throw a newborn child into the sea rather than maintain it. Furthermore women have the right to claim a divorce; they do this themselves whenever they wish. There is also an artificial make-up for the eyes: when they use it beauty never fades; on the contrary, it increases in men and women as well.

This goes to show how much opinion could color the reports of eyewitnesses. Although you wouldn't guess it from al-Tartushi's description, Hedeby was actually a very prosperous trading center. But al-Tartushi was from Córdoba, the most refined and sophisticated city in western Europe. We can take that into account as we read his comment on music in Hedeby: "I have never heard more horrible singing . . . it is like a growl coming out of their throats, like the barking of dogs, only much more beastly."

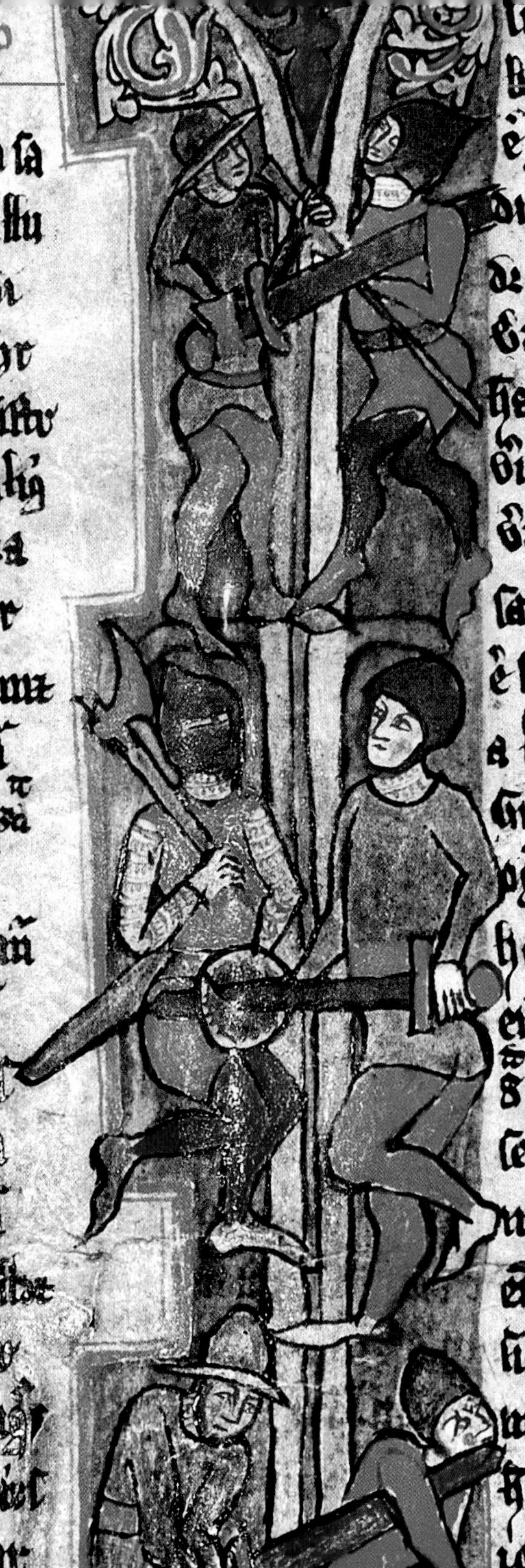

The END of an ERA

THE LATE TENTH CENTURY WAS A TIME OF TRANSITION AND upheaval for many in northern Europe. With Scandinavian kings asserting more power, there was more competition for the throne and more conflict between kings. The authority of local chiefs was eroding, so these men were seeking ways to maintain their wealth and influence. In Russia, too, rulers were increasing their control, greatly reducing Swedish opportunities in the east. With the dwindling availability of Arab silver, and new sources of silver in Europe emerging, trade patterns and the economy were also changing. As at the beginning of the Viking Age, there were many Scandinavians looking for instant fame and fortune. Now Danes, Norwegians, and Swedes alike turned their ambitions—and their longships—toward England.

FROM RAIDERS TO RULERS

In 980, Viking raids on England resumed with fierce intensity. Then in 991 Olaf Tryggvason led ninety-three ships in plundering the south-

Opposite page: A page from the fourteenth-century Icelandic manuscript *Flateyjarbók,* which contains a number of sagas, including the lives of Norwegian kings such as Olaf Tryggvason.

east of England. The English king, Aethelred, seemed unable to muster an adequate military response. Instead he resorted to bribery, as the *Anglo-Saxon Chronicle* recorded: "In this year it was first counselled that tribute be yielded to the Danishmen, because of the horrors they worked along the coasts. The first payment was ten thousand pounds."

Three years later Olaf was back, accompanied by King Svein Forkbeard of Denmark and a fleet of ninety-four ships. They first attacked London, then pillaged along the southern coast until Aethelred and his counselors decided once more to pay them to leave. The tribute this time was a full winter's provisions and sixteen thousand pounds of silver. The *Anglo-Saxon Chronicle*'s entry for the year concludes, "Olaf then promised him [Aethelred]—and also did as he promised— that he would never again come to the English people in enmity." He returned to Norway with his loot, which helped him to win the crown of Norway the next year.

Olaf's agreement to leave England in peace certainly didn't stop other Vikings. If anything, they were even more tempted to seek their fortunes there, since it was becoming ever more common for the English to pay them to stop raiding. In 1002 Aethelred bought off the latest group of raiders with the huge sum of 24,000 pounds. A few months later, believing there was a Scandinavian plot against him, he ordered all Danes in England killed. Although we don't know how thoroughly this command was carried out, we do know that one of the dead was Gunnhild, who had been captured along with her husband when he was raiding in England the previous year. Gunnhild was the sister of Svein Forkbeard.

Aethelred was nicknamed Unraed, Old English for "uncounseled" or "badly advised," but he's often been called Aethelred the Unready. This portrait is taken from one of the coins he issued during his reign.

In revenge, Svein led a series of fierce raids in 1003 and 1004. Bands of Vikings attacked England nearly every year following. Some of these raids seem to have been very well-organized operations. Aethelred tried to end them by paying the Danes ever larger amounts, peaking at 48,000 pounds in 1012. His efforts proved useless. In 1013 Svein himself returned to England at the head of his fleet. Aethelred fled to Normandy, and Svein was acknowledged king of England. He died only two months later, and his men named his son Cnut (or Canute) as his successor.

For two years Cnut battled Aethelred and then his son, Edmund. When Edmund died in 1016, Cnut took the English throne without resistance. Three years later he became king of Denmark as well. In 1028 he gained much of Norway and soon extended his influence into Sweden. Cnut's empire was the largest realm ever ruled by a Viking. It was also one of the best governed, at least in England, where Cnut lived most of the rest of his life. Even though he had been an invader, he was accepted as the country's lawful king. He had become a Christian in 1013, afterward pleasing the English people by making many donations to churches and monasteries. Best of all, England was at peace throughout Cnut's reign.

Cnut and his queen, Emma of Normandy, present a gold cross to a church in Winchester, England.

CHANGING WAYS

In 1027 Cnut went to Rome to attend the coronation of the new German emperor. As a Christian and the ruler of a sea-spanning empire, Cnut had become a full participant in mainstream European life. The same thing—although on a less grand scale—was happening to his fellow Scandinavians. The main reason was Christianity, which had been

THE OLD BELIEFS

TRADITIONAL NORSE RELIGION HONORED MANY DEITIES. The three greatest gods were Odin, Thor, and Frey. Odin, called the All-Father and the High One, was concerned with war, poetry, and magic. His wife, Frigg, was a goddess of prophecy and the home. Thor, armed with his mighty hammer, protected humankind both on land and sea. He was also the god of storms. Frey looked after the rain and sunshine that were necessary for the growth of crops. People called upon him, according to Snorri Sturluson, "for fruitful seasons and for peace." His sister, Freyja, shared these qualities, and was also a powerful goddess of love and magic.

Frey and Freyja were closely associated with nature spirits called elves. Some elves were thought of as guardians of particular farms and families; Norse housewives commonly made offerings of food to them. Judging by the records that have come down to us, the making of offerings was one of the main forms of worship in the Viking world. When meat was offered, the animal had to be killed in a special way that dedicated it to the gods (although worshippers, too, would share in the meat). Snorri Sturluson wrote that Odin himself decreed three annual sacrificial feasts: "there should be a sacrifice at the beginning of winter for a successful year, and at midwinter for regeneration, and a third in summer which was a sacrifice for victory."

Above: This bronze statue of Thor with his hammer was made around the year 1000 and is less than three inches tall—small enough to be held in a worshipper's hand.

the dominant religion of most of western Europe for centuries and was in many ways the heart of medieval European culture.

The church began to send missionaries to Scandinavia during the 800s. Norse raiders, traders, and settlers also encountered Christianity abroad. Through formal and informal contacts, it made slow inroads, often peacefully coexisting with native beliefs. Sometimes the new beliefs and the old coexisted within one person. For example, a ninth-century woman was buried in Hedeby, Denmark, wearing both a Christian cross and a pendant in the shape of a hammer, symbol of the god Thor. The *Book of Settlements* tells us that an Icelander known as Helgi the Skinny "believed in Christ, but prayed to Thor on sea-journeys and in tough situations."

Many Norse converts sincerely embraced Christianity's teachings. Many others seem to have accepted it primarily for its usefulness. Scandinavian merchants quickly learned that adopting at least some aspects of Christianity was good for trade—Christians preferred to do business with other Christians. Scandinavian kings found that the same was true in international relations—Christian rulers negotiated more favorable agreements (including marriages between royal families) with other Christian rulers. Norse monarchs also realized that the strong organization and power structure of the church would support their authority and help them extend it.

Once a king became Christian, his subjects generally had to follow, although conversion did not always happen willingly or peacefully. For

A Swedish rock carving may portray a couple who have embraced Christianity, symbolized by the cross held by the man.

instance, Olaf Haraldsson (later Saint Olaf), who ruled Norway from 1015 to 1030, ordered chieftains who did not accept Christianity to be blinded or outlawed. To the common people Olaf offered the choice of being baptized, exiled, or killed.

Different conditions prevailed in Iceland, where there had been Christians since the early years of settlement. Most were slaves or freedmen and freedwomen from Ireland or Scotland. Some of the leading Norse colonists had also embraced Christianity, among them Aud the Deep-Minded. (The situation was similar in Greenland, where the first Christian settler was Erik the Red's wife, Thjodhild.) By the year 1000, however, conflicts between Christians and non-Christians had reached a point where many Icelanders felt something needed to be done. At the Althing that year, both sides appealed to the lawspeaker, Thorgeir, for arbitration.

After meditating for a day and a night, Thorgeir said, "It seems to me good sense . . . that we should seek a middle course, so that we all have one law and one custom; because if we divide the law, we will divide the peace." Then, says an early Icelandic history, "Thorgeir declared the law, that all unbaptised people in the land should become Christian and be baptised." The decision must have been a surprise, since Thorgeir himself followed the old faith. But knowing how much Iceland's reliance on imports required close relations with other countries, most of which were Christian or becoming Christian, Thorgeir's choice was one that made, as he said, "good sense."

THE LAST OF THE VIKINGS

After Cnut's death in 1035, his empire collapsed, and England and Scandinavia entered another period of turmoil. It was during this time that King Olaf Haraldsson's half-brother Harald served as a mercenary in Russia and then in the Varangian Guard. In 1044 Harald returned to Scandinavia (having married a Russian princess on his way back) and began his two-year fight to take the throne of Norway. He dealt so harshly with the Norwegian chiefs who resisted his authority that he was given the nickname Hardradi, "hard ruler." He then set about conquering Denmark, but it took him twenty years of warfare with the Danish king (Cnut's nephew), during which thousands of men died.

With Norway and Denmark under his power, Harald Hardradi felt he had a claim on the rest of Cnut's empire and turned his sights on England. In secret he prepared a fleet of three hundred ships. With each ship probably carrying about thirty men, Harald's army numbered around nine thousand. They landed in northern England in September 1066, and Harald quickly took the city of York.

The English king, Harold Godwinsson, had been in the south, expecting an invasion by William, Duke of Normandy. When he heard about Hardradi's landing, he marched his army north. At noon on September 25 he surprised the Norwegian army outside York at Stamford Bridge. *King Harald's Saga* described Hardradi watching the English approach: "And the closer the army came, the greater it grew, and their glittering weapons sparkled like a field of broken ice."

The two kings met. Harald of Norway demanded land. Harold of England swore he would give him only enough to be buried in. The battle began, and raged through the day, both sides fighting ferociously. Then, according to the saga, Harald Hardradi "fell into . . . a fury of battle":

He rushed forward ahead of his troops, hewing with both hands. Neither helmet nor armour could withstand him, and everyone in his path gave way before him. It looked then as if the English were on the point of being routed. . . . But now King Harald . . . was struck in the throat by an arrow, and that was his death-wound.

The English won the day; so many of the invaders were killed that only twenty-four ships were needed to take the survivors home to Nor-

In a scene from the Bayeux Tapestry, William of Normandy's fleet nears the English coast.

way. But Harold Godwinsson's troubles weren't over. Only three days after the death of Harald Hardradi, William of Normandy and his 10,000-man army landed in southern England. Godwinsson once again force-marched his men to battle. The two armies had their historic confrontation at Hastings on October 14, 1066. The *Anglo-Saxon Chronicle* sums up the result: "There king Harold was killed. . . . The French held the field."

The Viking Age is said to have begun in England, with the raid on Lindisfarne in 793. It can also be said to have ended in England, with the events of 1066, which were both significant and symbolic. Harald Hardradi, whose life was one of Viking adventure, was defeated by an English king who was the grandson of a Danish Viking, who in turn was defeated by a direct descendant of the Northman Rollo. But Rollo's great-great-grandson William was not regarded as a Northman or Viking. He was French.

The Normans weren't the only Scandinavian population who had blended in with the people they settled among, adopting their language

and customs. The same thing had happened in Russia. For that matter, it had happened in England's Danelaw.

In Ireland, Viking power had been dwindling, although distinct Scandinavian communities remained in the cities. Most of the Northmen were now Christians, though, and they hired themselves out as mercenaries to feuding Irish kings far more often than they conducted raids on their own behalf.

Raiders still sailed from the Norse settlements in the Scottish islands, and sometimes even from Norway itself, into the thirteenth century. But the great outpouring of Scandinavian warriors, merchants, and colonists was over. By the second half of the twelfth century, Denmark, Norway, and Sweden were each united under a single ruler and were fully involved in the culture and politics of western Europe. Looking to the future, the Scandinavian countries were well on their way to becoming the nations we know today.

A Norman kills an English soldier. After the Battle of Hastings, William of Normandy became King William I of England, also known as William the Conqueror.

KEY DATES IN VIKING HISTORY

793 Viking raid on monastery at Lindisfarne in the English kingdom of Northumbria

794 Viking raid on monastery at Jarrow, Northumbria

799 Viking raid in western Frankia

802, 806 Viking raids on monastery at Iona

834 first of three Viking raids on Dorestad, Frisia

836 twenty-five shiploads of Vikings attack the English kingdom of Wessex

841 Vikings establish a *longphort* at Dublin, Ireland

842 Vikings overwinter near the mouth of the Loire River in Frankia

844 a Viking fleet raids the Iberian cities of Lisbon, Cadiz, and Seville

845 100 Viking ships sail up the Seine River to Paris

850 Vikings overwinter on an island in southeastern England

mid-800s Swedish warriors and merchants known as Rus dominate Kiev and Novgorod

859—862 Bjorn Ironside and Hastein lead a Viking expedition into the Mediterranean

860 approximate date of first Rus raid on Constantinople

860s settlement of Iceland begins

866 the Great Army, made up mostly of Danes, invades England

867 the Great Army captures the city of York, capital of Northumbria

876 Danish commander Halfdan distributes Northumbrian farmland to his men

886 Alfred the Great cedes English lands known as the Danelaw to Vikings

902 Alfred's son Edward begins conquest of Danelaw; Norwegian Vikings driven out of Dublin

907 Rus raid on Constantinople

911 Frankish king gives lands to Viking leader Rollo

914 a Viking army conquers Brittany

915 Vikings return to Dublin

917 Edward and his sister Aethelflaed bring most of Danelaw under English rule

922 Arab diplomat Ibn Fadlan meets Rus along the Volga River

930 Icelanders establish a national assembly, the Althing

939 the Bretons drive the Vikings out of Brittany

941, 944 Rus raids on Constantinople

954 the last Viking king of York, Erik Bloodaxe,
is killed in battle

986 Erik the Red leads the settlement of
Greenland; Bjarni Herjolfsson sights
North America

991 Olaf Tryggvason leads 93 ships in plundering
the southeast of England

994 Olaf Tryggvason and Danish king Svein Forkbeard
attack London

995 Olaf Tryggvason becomes king of Norway

1000 Leif Eriksson leads first Scandinavian exploration of North America;
Iceland chooses Christianity as its official religion

1002 king of England pays huge tribute to Vikings, then orders all Danes in
England killed

1013 Svein Forkbeard conquers England, dies, and is succeeded by his son
Cnut; Cnut becomes a Christian

1015 Olaf Haraldsson becomes king of Norway and begins to force his
subjects to convert to Christianity

1019 Cnut becomes king of Denmark as well as England

1028 Cnut adds much of Norway to his realm

1035 death of Cnut

1036 Ingvar leads expedition from Sweden to somewhere east of the Caspian Sea

1046 Harald Hardradi becomes king of Norway, begins conquest of Denmark

1066 Harald Hardradi invades England, is defeated at the Battle of Stamford
Bridge on September 25; William of Normandy invades England, defeats
the English at the Battle of Hastings on October 14

A hoard of coins and jewelry from mid-ninth-century Birka, Sweden

GLOSSARY

Althing The national assembly of Iceland during the Viking Age. After Iceland came under Norwegian and then Danish rule (in 1262 and 1380) the Althing became a court of law, till 1800. It was restored as the nation's parliament when Iceland regained its independence in 1944.

Britain The island now occupied by the nations of England, Wales, and Scotland. At the beginning of the Viking Age there were four English kingdoms (Wessex in the south, Mercia in the center, East Anglia in the east, and Northumbria in the north) and two main Welsh kingdoms (Gwynedd in the north and Dyfed in the south). What is now Scotland included the Welsh-speaking kingdom of Strathclyde in the southeast, north of that the Irish-speaking kingdom of Dalríada, and north of that the ancient kingdom of the Picts.

Byzantine Empire The Greek-speaking eastern half of the Roman Empire, with its capital at Constantinople. During most of the Viking Age it was comprised mainly of what are now Greece and Turkey.

deciduous Refers to trees that lose their leaves in the fall.

dirhem A silver coin; the basic unit of currency in the medieval Muslim world.

fjord A narrow waterway where the sea flows inland between cliffs or mountains.

heathen and **pagan** Terms used to describe followers of traditional, pre-Christian religions and their beliefs and practices.

high seat A central bench in a Norse house, reserved for the house's owner; it might be framed by carved wooden pillars, which also helped support the roof.

Iberia The peninsula occupied by modern Spain and Portugal. During the Viking Age most of Iberia was under Arab rule and was known as al-Andalus.

longphort An Irish word for a fortified landing place for Viking ships.

marten A large weasel-like animal with thick, dark fur.

Middle Ages The period of European history from about 500 to about 1500.

Norse The name scholars generally prefer to use for Viking Age Scandinavians when they were not taking part in Viking expeditions.

Saami People of arctic and subarctic Norway, Sweden, Finland, and Russia, who traditionally made much of their living as reindeer herders and hunters. They have also been known as Lapps or Laplanders.

saga A long story in prose written down in medieval Scandinavia or Iceland. Some sagas related myths and legends, but many were histories, telling of important events and of Vikings, settlers, explorers, kings, poets, and other notable people.

Slavic Refers to Slavic languages and to the peoples of central and eastern Europe who speak them. The Slavic languages spoken during the Viking Age included early forms of Polish, Russian, Ukrainian, and Bulgarian.

taiga Subarctic forest land, where the main plants are coniferous trees—cone-bearing evergreens such as pine, spruce, and fir.

tundra Land where the soil is permanently frozen below the surface, allowing only short-lived grasses and similar plants to grow during the brief summer.

Viking Age A common name for the period during which Scandinavian raiders were most active in the British Isles and continental Europe, usually dated from 793 to 1066.

FOR MORE INFORMATION

BOOKS

Berger, Melvin, and Gilda Berger. *The Real Vikings: Craftsmen, Traders, and Fearsome Raiders*. Washington, DC: National Geographic, 2003.

Gallagher, Jim. *The Viking Explorers*. Philadelphia: Chelsea House, 2001.

Grant, Neil. *The Vikings*. New York: Oxford University Press, 1998.

Gravett, Christopher. *Going to War in Viking Times*. Danbury, CT: Franklin Watts, 2001.

Hinds, Kathryn. *Cultures of the Past: The Vikings*. New York: Benchmark Books, 1998.

Lassieur, Allison. *The Vikings*. San Diego, CA: Lucent Books, 2001.

Philip, Neil. *Odin's Family: Myths of the Vikings*. New York: Orchard Books, 1996.

Rees, Rosemary. *The Vikings*. Chicago, IL: Heinemann Library, 2002.

Schomp, Virginia. *Myths of the World: The Norsemen*. New York: Marshall Cavendish Benchmark, 2008.

Schomp, Virginia. *The Vikings*. New York: Scholastic, 2005.

WEB SITES

BBC. *Ancient History: Vikings.*
http://www.bbc.co.uk/history/ancient/vikings/

Jorvik Viking Centre. *Vikings.*
http://www.jorvik-viking-centre.co.uk/vikings1.htm

National Museum of Natural History. *Vikings: The North Atlantic Saga.*
http://www.mnh.si.edu/vikings/start.html

NOVA Online. *The Vikings.*
http://www.pbs.org/wgbh/nova/vikings/

Parks Canada. *L'Anse aux Meadows National Historic Site.*
   http://www.pc.gc.ca/lhn-nhs/nl/meadows/index_e.asp
Viking Ship Museum. *The Sea Stallion from Glendalough:*
   The Longship-Past and Present.
   http://www.vikingeskibsmuseet.dk/index.php?id = 647&L = 1

SELECTED BIBLIOGRAPHY

Almgren, Bertil, ed. *The Viking.* New York: Crescent Books, 1978.

Chartrand, R., et al. *The Vikings: Voyagers of Discovery and Plunder.*
   New York: Osprey, 2006.

Fitzhugh, William W., and Elisabeth I. Ward, eds. *Vikings: The North*
   Atlantic Saga. Washington, DC: Smithsonian Institution Press, 2000.

Fletcher, Richard. *The Barbarian Conversion: From Paganism to Chris-*
   tianity. New York: Henry Holt, 1997.

Graham-Campbell, James, ed. *Cultural Atlas of the Viking World.* New
   York: Facts on File, 1994.

Haywood, John. *Encyclopaedia of the Viking Age.* New York: Thames
   and Hudson, 2000.

Kennedy, Hugh. *Mongols, Huns, and Vikings: Nomads at War.* London:
   Cassell, 2002.

Magnusson, Magnus. *Vikings!* New York: E. P. Dutton, 1980.

Marsden, John. *The Fury of the Northmen: Saints, Shrines and Sea-*
   Raiders in the Viking Age, AD 793–878. New York: St. Martin's
   Press, 1993.

McCullough, David Willis, ed. *Chronicles of the Barbarians: Firsthand*
   Accounts of Pillage and Conquest, From the Ancient World to the
   Fall of Constantinople. New York: Times Books, 1998.

Savage, Anne, trans. *The Anglo-Saxon Chronicles.* New York: St. Martin's Press, 1983.

Sawyer, Peter, ed. *The Oxford Illustrated History of the Vikings.* New York: Oxford University Press, 1997.

SOURCES FOR QUOTATIONS

Chapter 1

p. 9 "Dire portents": Graham-Campbell, *Cultural Atlas of the Viking World*, p. 122.

p. 10 "The pagans": Marsden, *The Fury of the Northmen*, p. 42.

p. 10 "never before": Magnusson, *Vikings!*, p. 34.

p. 14 "That tribute consists": Fitzhugh, *Vikings*, p. 49.

p. 21 "King Olaf": Kennedy, *Mongols, Huns and Vikings*, pp. 182–183.

Chapter 2

p. 23 "he had more": Chartrand, *The Vikings*, pp. 15–16.

p. 24 "the pagans first": Marsden, *The Fury of the Northmen*, p. 68.

p. 25 "Bitter is the wind": Magnusson, *Vikings!*, p. 152.

p. 25 "one of their leaders": Marsden, *The Fury of the Northmen*, p. 56.

p. 26 "The Danes attacked": Sawyer, *The Oxford Illustrated History of the Vikings*, p. 23.

p. 26 "heathen men" and "fought with": Savage, *The Anglo-Saxon Chronicles*, p. 83.

p. 27 "the Northmen with a hundred": McCullough, *Chronicles of the Barbarians*, p. 215.

p. 27 "coming to the ocean": ibid., p. 216.

p. 28 "Pagans still": Sawyer, *The Oxford Illustrated History of the Vikings*, p. 88.

p. 28 "After they had been": ibid., p. 88.

p. 29 "It is related" and "One summer Harald": Graham-Campbell, *Cultural Atlas of the Viking World*, p. 151.

p. 30 "a great heathen force": Savage, *The Anglo-Saxon Chronicles*, p. 92.

p. 31 "they were ploughing": ibid., p. 96.

p. 33 "The number of ships": Graham-Campbell, *Cultural Atlas of the Viking World*, p. 142.

Chapter 3

p. 35 "He said that the land": Fitzhugh, *Vikings*, p. 31.

p. 35 "set of small islands": ibid., p. 154.

p. 36 "in the days": Graham-Campbell, *Cultural Atlas of the Viking World*, p. 166.

p. 37 "The fjord teemed": Magnusson, *Vikings!*, p. 188.

p. 37 "butter dripped": ibid., p. 188.

p. 38 quotations in the story of Aud the Deep-minded from *The Book of the Settlement of Iceland*, translated by T. Ellwood, London, 1898. Online at http://www.northvegr.org/lore/landnamabok/011.php

p. 40 "Fourteen reached it": Sawyer, *The Oxford Illustrated History of the Vikings*, p. 118.

p. 41 "Wise men say": ibid., p. 115.

p. 43 "There was great discussion": Fitzhugh, *Vikings*, p. 219.

p. 44 "hired himself": ibid., p. 221.

p. 45 "taking with them": ibid., p. 221.

p. 45 "Discussion soon began": ibid., p. 221.

p. 46 "There was now much talk": ibid., pp. 219–220.

Chapter 4

p. 49 "The Danish pirates": McCullough, *Chronicles of the Barbarians*, p. 217.

p. 51 "There arose strife": Magnusson, *Vikings!*, pp. 110–111.

p. 52 "set himself up": ibid., p. 116.

p. 55 "They regard loyalty": Chartrand, *The Vikings*, p. 56.

p. 56 "I have never seen": McCullough, *Chronicles of the Barbarians*, p. 223.

p. 57 "You take the people": ibid., p. 228.

p. 57 "Tola had this stone": Almgren, *The Viking*, p. 150.

p. 58 "a long upright" and "O my Lord": McCullough, *Chronicles of the Barbarians*, p. 224.

p. 58 "I want" and "Then he takes": Almgren, *The Viking*, p. 139.

p. 59 "They fight with the Slavs": Magnusson, *Vikings!*, p. 117.

p. 59 "They hold a feast": Almgren, *The Viking*, p. 59.

p. 59 "I have never heard": Magnusson, *Vikings!*, p. 68.

Chapter 5

p. 62 "In this year": Savage, *The Anglo-Saxon Chronicles*, p. 144.

p. 62 "Olaf then promised": ibid., p. 145.

p. 64 "for fruitful seasons": Magnusson, *Vikings!*, p. 13.

p. 64 "there should be": Graham-Campbell, *Cultural Atlas of the Viking World*, p. 114.

p. 65 "believed in Christ": ibid., p. 115.

p. 66 "It seems to me" and "Thorgeir declared": Magnusson, *Vikings!*, p. 203.

p. 67 "And the closer": ibid., p. 310.

p. 67 "fell into" and "He rushed forward": ibid., p. 310.

p. 68 "There King Harold": Savage, *The Anglo-Saxon Chronicles*, p. 195.

INDEX

ABOUT THE AUTHOR

KATHRYN HINDS grew up near Rochester, New York. She studied music and writing at Barnard College, and went on to do graduate work in comparative literature and medieval studies at the City University of New York. She has written more than forty books for young people, including *Everyday Life in Medieval Europe* and the books in the series LIFE IN THE MEDIEVAL MUSLIM WORLD, LIFE IN ELIZABETHAN ENGLAND, LIFE IN ANCIENT EGYPT, LIFE IN THE ROMAN EMPIRE, and LIFE IN THE RENAISSANCE. Kathryn lives in the north Georgia mountains with her husband, their son, and an assortment of cats and dogs. When she is not reading or writing, she enjoys dancing, gardening, knitting, playing music, and taking walks in the woods. Visit Kathryn online at www.kathrynhinds.com